VOL. 63

HAL•LEONARD®
GUITAR PLAY-ALONG

AUDIO ACCESS INCLUDED

PLAYBACK+
Speed • Pitch • Balance • Loop

CREEDENCE CLEARWATER REVIVAL

To access audio visit:
www.halleonard.com/mylibrary

Enter Code
7846-6663-4000-3930

Cover photo by Michael Putland / Retna

Tracking, mixing, and mastering by
Jake Johnson & Bill Maynard at Paradyme Productions
All guitars by Doug Boduch
Bass by Tom McGirr
Piano by Warren Wiegratz
Drums by Scott Schroedl

ISBN 978-1-4234-1383-7

T0057636

Visit Hal Leonard Online at www.halleonard.com

In Australia Contact:
Hal Leonard Australia Pty. Ltd.
4 Lentara Court
Cheltenham, Victoria, 3192 Australia
Email: ausadmin@halleonard.com

HAL•LEONARD®
7777 W. BLUEMOUND RD. P.O. BOX 13819
MILWAUKEE, WISCONSIN 53213

Guitar Notation Legend

THE MUSICAL STAFF shows pitches and rhythms and is divided by bar lines into measures. Pitches are named after the first seven letters of the alphabet.

TABLATURE graphically represents the guitar fingerboard. Each horizontal line represents a string, and each number represents a fret.

4th string, 2nd fret   1st & 2nd strings open, played together   open D chord

HALF-STEP BEND: Strike the note and bend up 1/2 step.

WHOLE-STEP BEND: Strike the note and bend up one step.

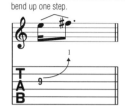

GRACE NOTE BEND: Strike the note and bend up as indicated. The first note does not take up any time.

SLIGHT (MICROTONE) BEND: Strike the note and bend up 1/4 step.

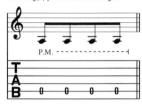

BEND AND RELEASE: Strike the note and bend up as indicated, then release back to the original note. Only the first note is struck.

PRE-BEND: Bend the note as indicated, then strike it.

VIBRATO: The string is vibrated by rapidly bending and releasing the note with the fretting hand.

PALM MUTING: The note is partially muted by the pick hand lightly touching the string(s) just before the bridge.

HAMMER-ON: Strike the first (lower) note with one finger, then sound the higher note (on the same string) with another finger by fretting it without picking.

PULL-OFF: Place both fingers on the notes to be sounded. Strike the first note and without picking, pull the finger off to sound the second (lower) note.

LEGATO SLIDE: Strike the first note and then slide the same fret-hand finger up or down to the second note. The second note is not struck.

SHIFT SLIDE: Same as legato slide, except the second note is struck.

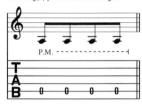

TRILL: Very rapidly alternate between the notes indicated by continuously hammering on and pulling off.

TAPPING: Hammer ("tap") the fret indicated with the pick-hand index or middle finger and pull off to the note fretted by the fret hand.

NATURAL HARMONIC: Strike the note while the fret-hand lightly touches the string directly over the fret indicated.

PINCH HARMONIC: The note is fretted normally and a harmonic is produced by adding the edge of the thumb or the tip of the index finger of the pick hand to the normal pick attack.

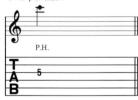

TREMOLO PICKING: The note is picked as rapidly and continuously as possible.

VIBRATO BAR DIVE AND RETURN: The pitch of the note or chord is dropped a specified number of steps (in rhythm) then returned to the original pitch.

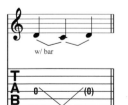

VIBRATO BAR SCOOP: Depress the bar just before striking the note, then quickly release the bar.

VIBRATO BAR DIP: Strike the note and then immediately drop a specified number of steps, then release back to the original pitch.

Additional Musical Definitions

(accent)	• Accentuate note (play it louder)	

(staccato)	• Play the note short

D.S. al Coda • Go back to the sign (𝄋), then play until the measure marked *"To Coda"*, then skip to the section labelled *"Coda."*

D.C. al Fine • Go back to the beginning of the song and play until the measure marked *"Fine"* (end).

Fill • Label used to identify a brief melodic figure which is to be inserted into the arrangement.

N.C. • No Chord

• Repeat measures between signs.

1. **2.** • When a repeated section has different endings, play the first ending only the first time and the second ending only the second time.

CREEDENCE CLEARWATER REVIVAL

CONTENTS

Bad Moon Rising

Words and Music by John Fogerty

Tune down 1 step:
(low to high) D-G-C-F-A-D

Intro

Moderately fast ♩ = 180

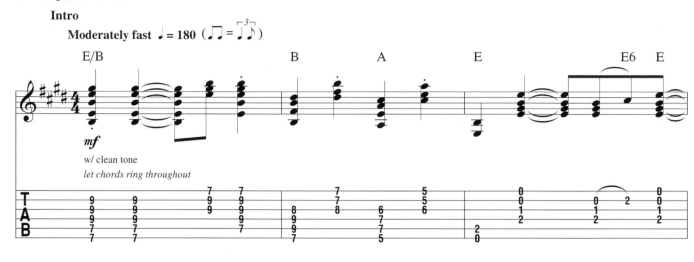

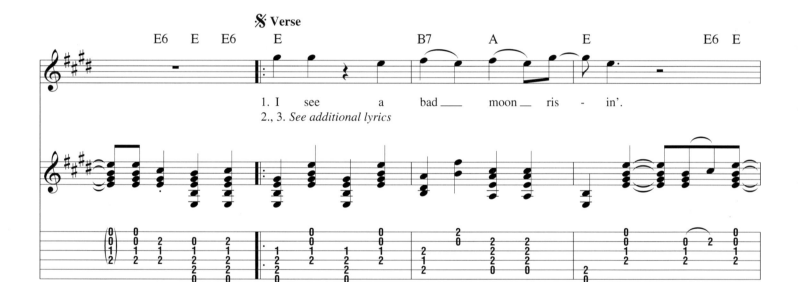

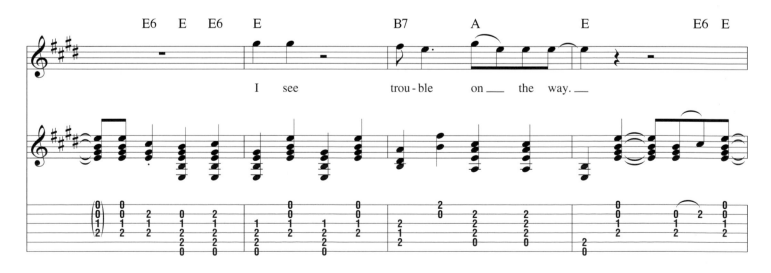

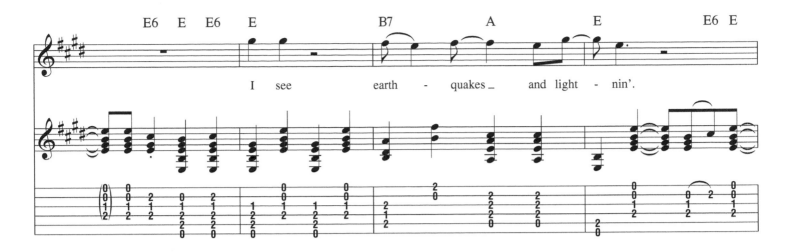

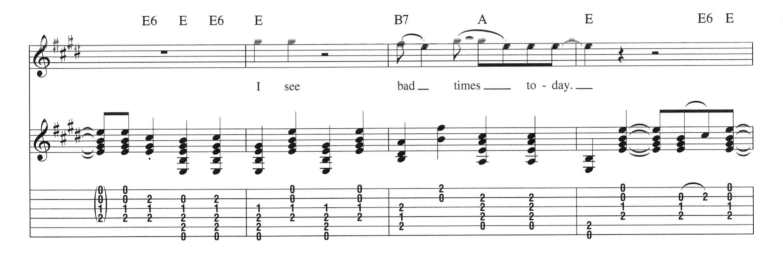

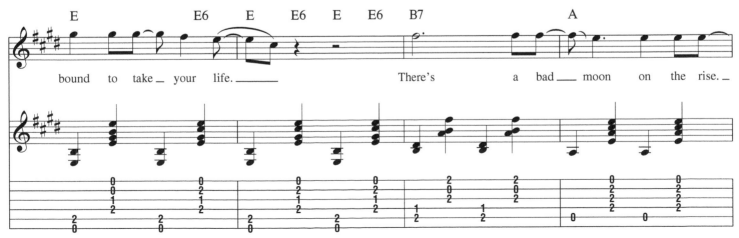

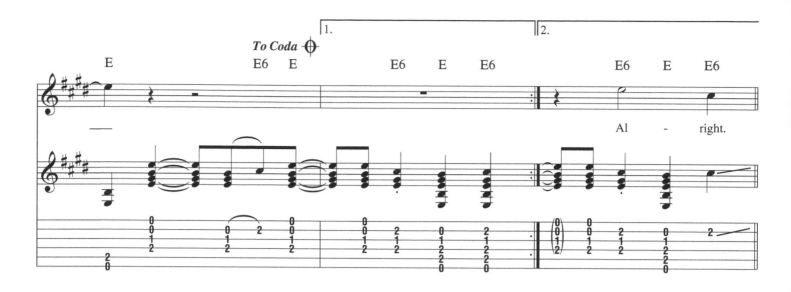

Al - right.

Guitar Solo

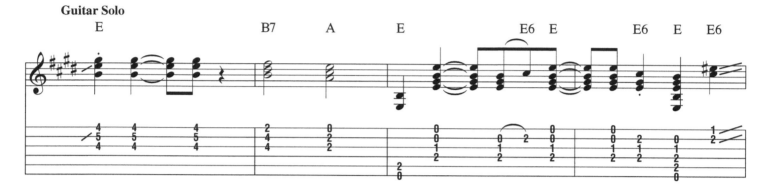

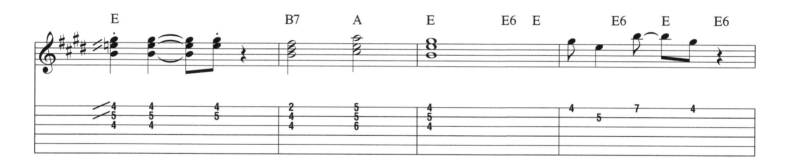

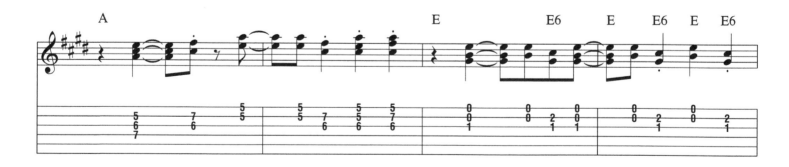

D.S. al Coda

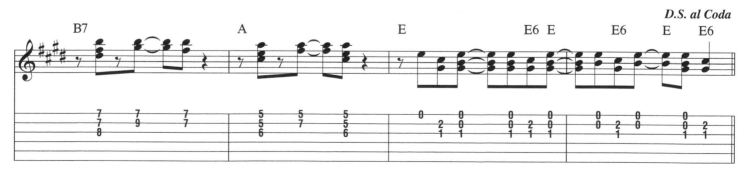

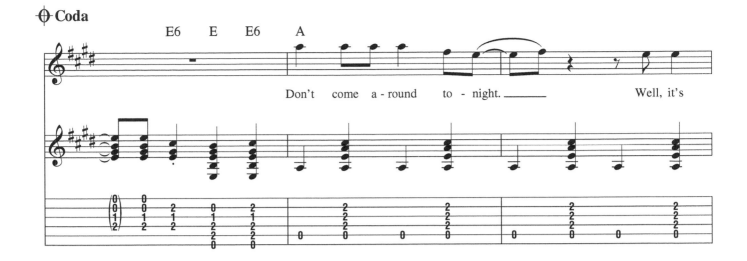

Coda

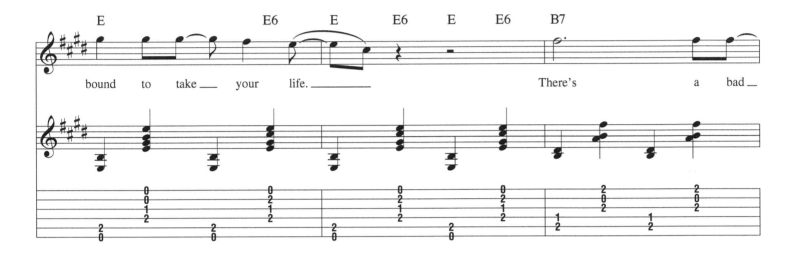

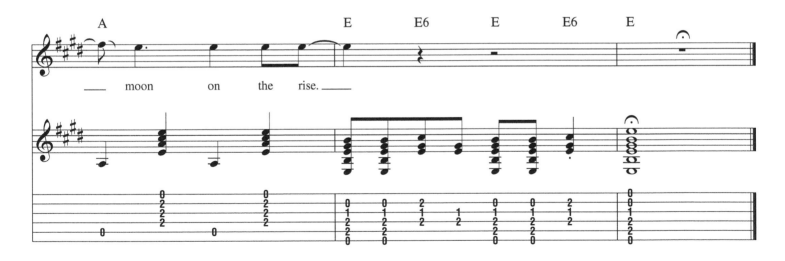

Additional Lyrics

2. I hear hurricanes a blowin'.
   I know the end is comin' soon.
   I fear rivers overflowin'.
   I hear the voice of rage and ruin.

3. Hope you got your things together.
   Hope you are quite prepared to die.
   Looks like we're in for nasty weather.
   One eye is taken for an eye. Well...

Born on the Bayou

Words and Music by John Fogerty

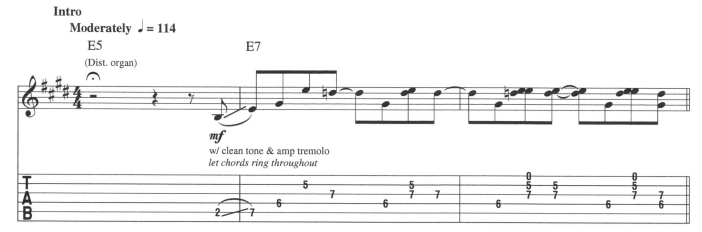

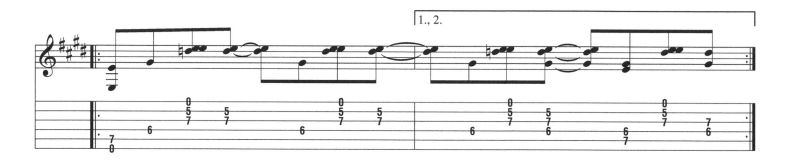

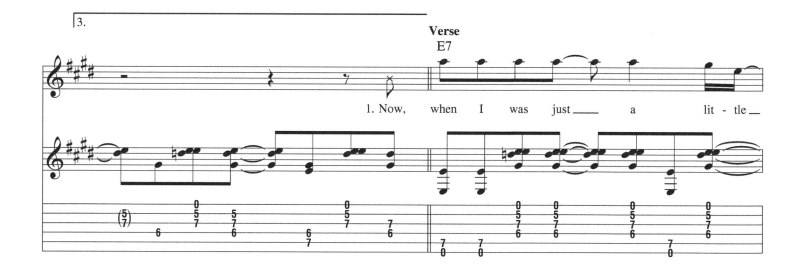

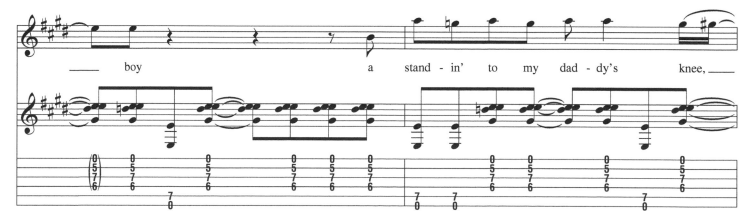

my pa-pa said, "Son, don't let____

the man____ get - cha,____ do____ what he done to me

'cause he - 'll get - cha,____

'cause he'll get-cha now, now.

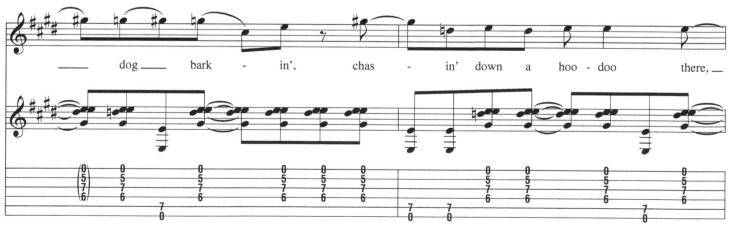

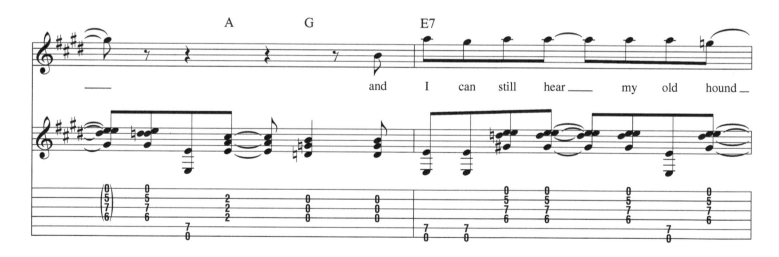

% **Verse**

E7

2. And (4.) I can re - mem - ber the Fourth ___

A   G   E7

___ of Ju - ly   a run-nin' through the back wood bare, ___

A   G   E7

___ and I can still hear ___ my old hound ___

___ dog ___ bark - in', chas - in' down a hoo - doo there, ___

10

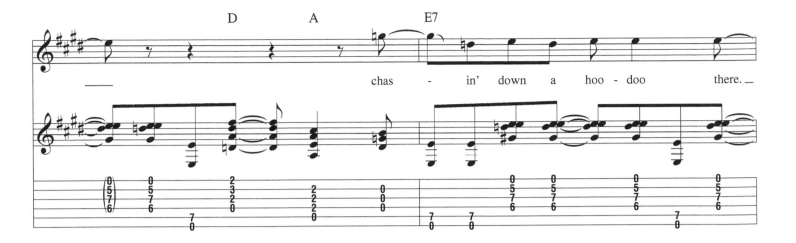

chas - in' down a hoo - doo there. __

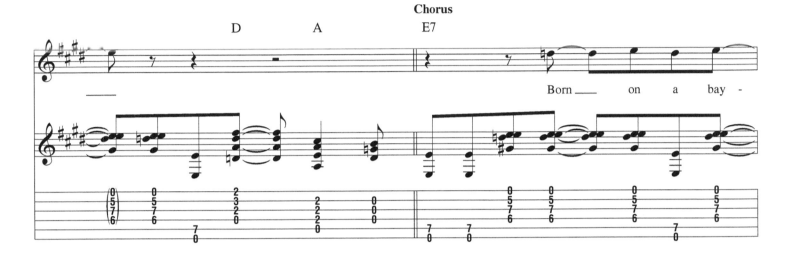

Born __ on a bay -

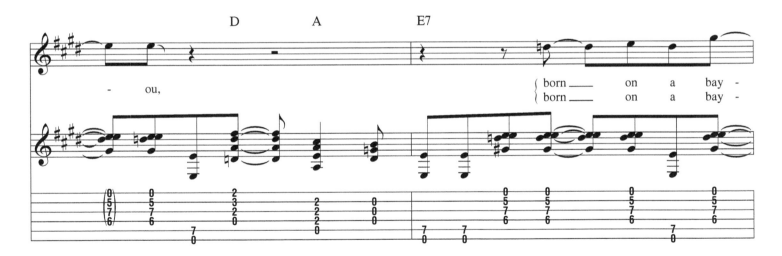

- ou, born __ on a bay -
born __ on a bay -

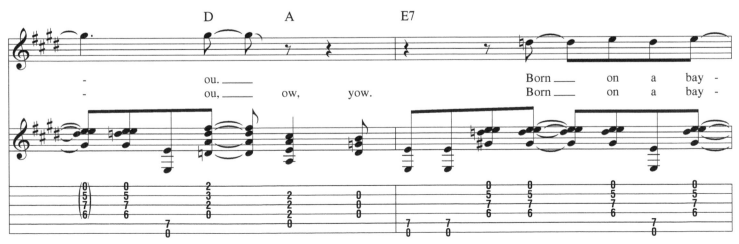

- ou. __ Born __ on a bay -
- ou, __ ow, yow. Born __ on a bay -

D   A   E7

- ou,   Lord,   Lord.
- ou.   Gon - na run,   go.   Doot,

Guitar Solo

E7

w/ slight dist.

let ring - - - - - - -⌐   *let ring -*

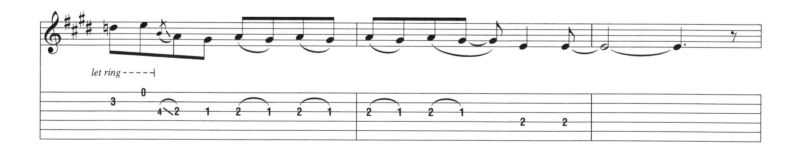

let ring - - - - -⌐

w/ fingers

let ring - - ⌐   *let ring - - ⌐*

Interlude

E7

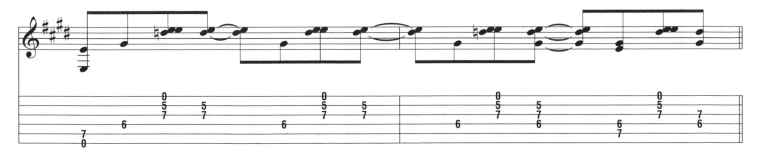

Verse

3. Wish I were back ___ on a bay - ou, roll -

- in' with some ___ Ca - jun ___ queen. A,

wish that I were ___ a fast ___ freight train ___ a just a

choog - lin' on ___ down to New Or - leans. ___

Chorus

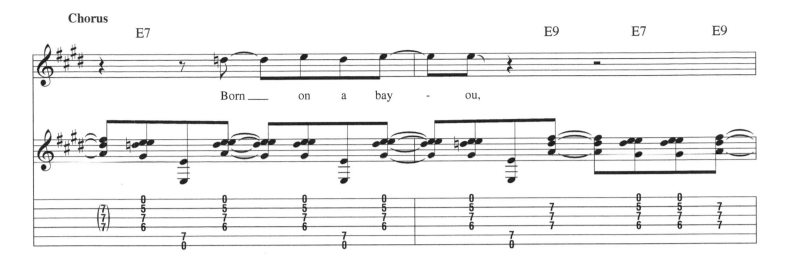

Born ___ on a bay - ou,

born ___ on the bay - ou, mm, mm,

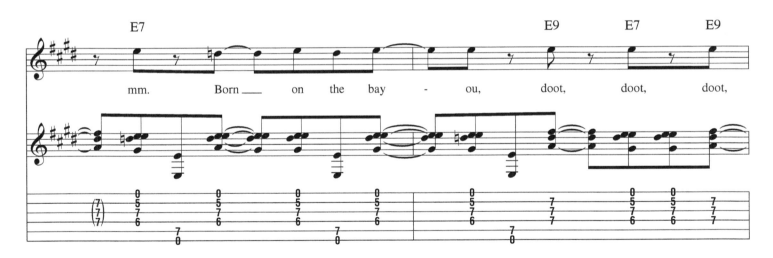

mm. Born ___ on the bay - ou, doot, doot, doot,

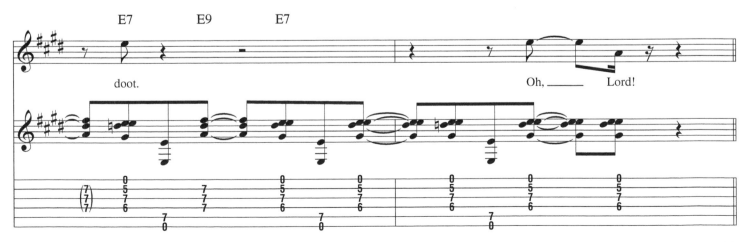

doot. Oh, ___ Lord!

Interlude

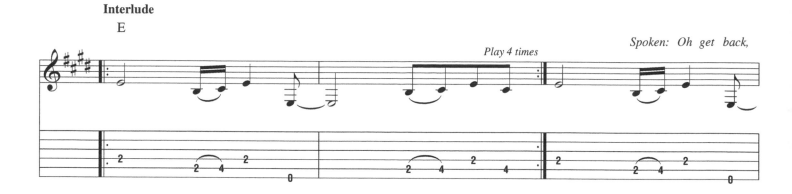

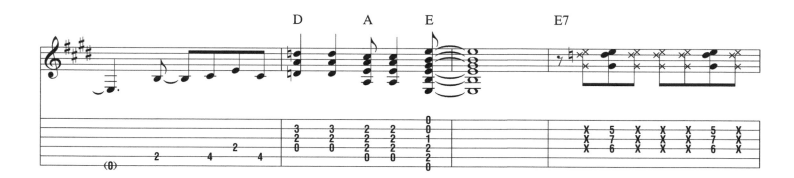

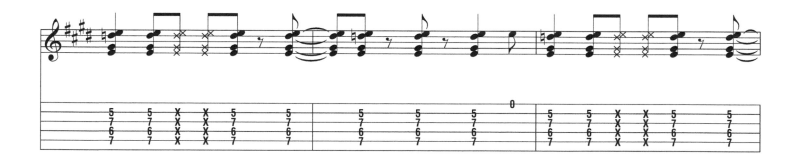

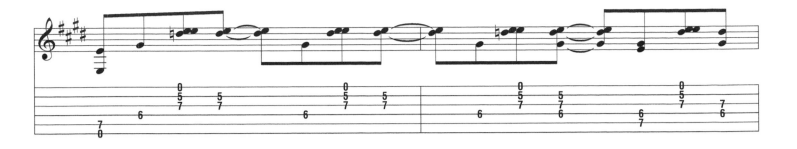

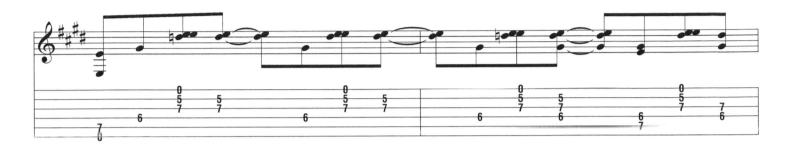

D.S. al Coda

4. Well,

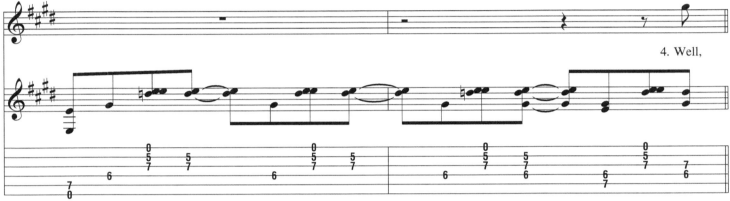

$\oplus$ **Coda**

Outro

E7

doot, doot, doot, ah.

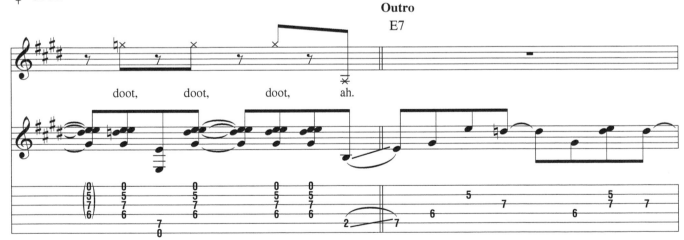

Repeat and fade

Down on the Corner

Words and Music by John Fogerty

1. Ear - ly   in   the   eve - nin'   just ___ a - bout   sup-per - time, ___
2., 3. *See additional lyrics*

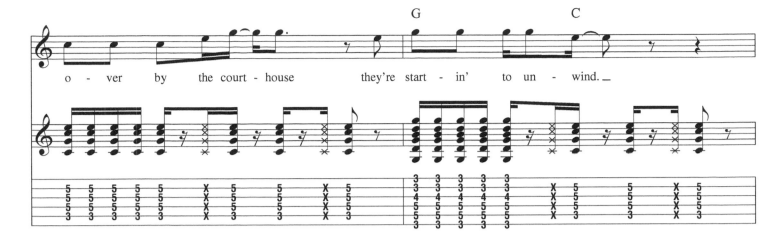

o - ver by the court - house they're start - in' to un - wind. __

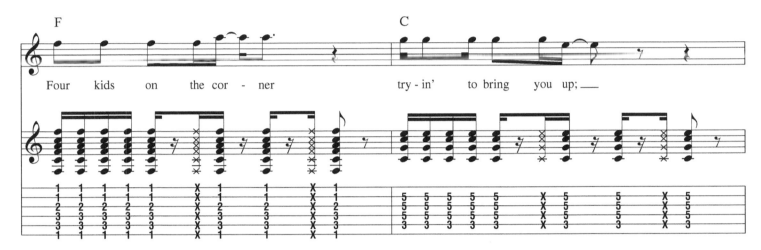

Four kids on the cor - ner try - in' to bring you up; ___

To Coda 2 $\oplus$

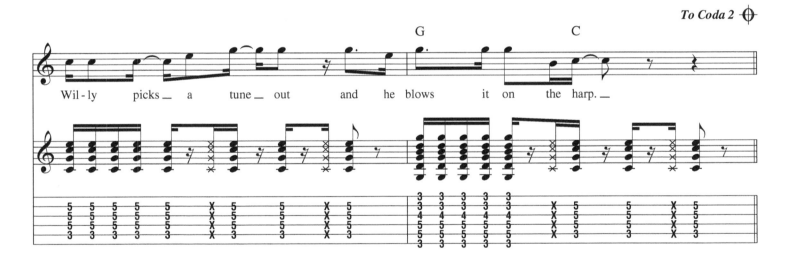

Wil - ly picks __ a tune __ out and he blows it on the harp. __

𝄉 **Chorus**

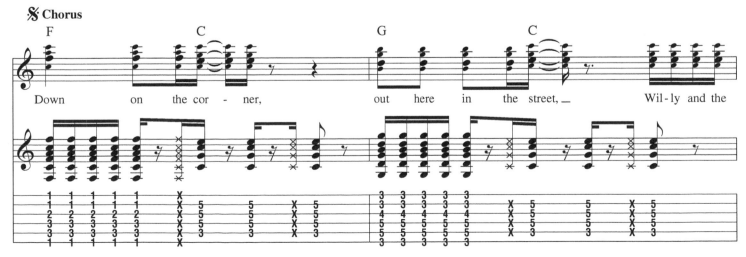

Down on the cor - ner, out here in the street, __ Wil - ly and the

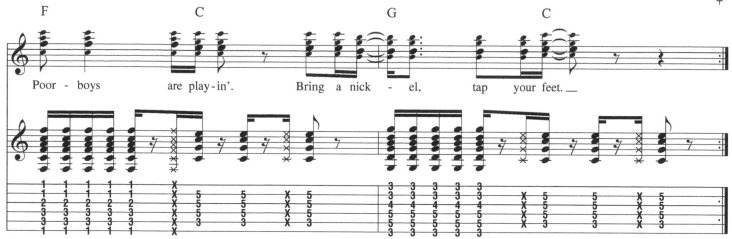

Poor - boys are play-in'. Bring a nick - el, tap your feet. __

Interlude

D.S. al Coda 1

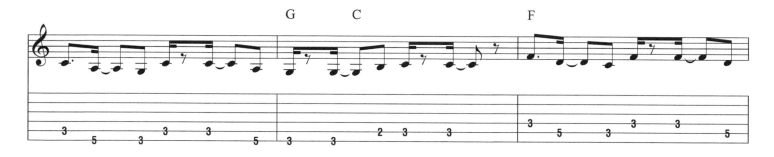

⊕ **Coda 1**

Interlude

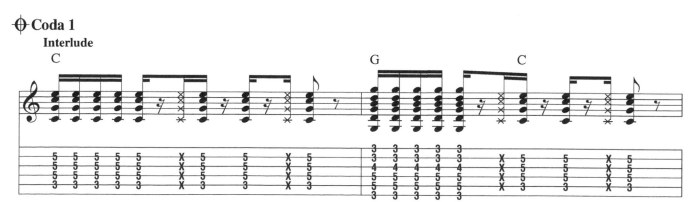

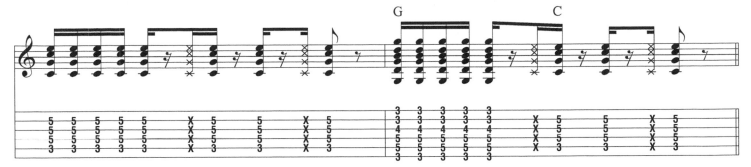

⊕ Coda 2

Outro-Chorus

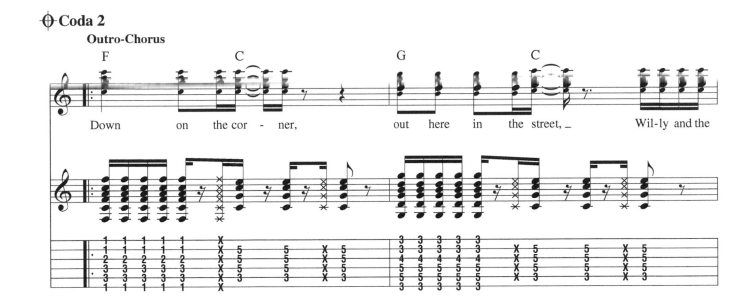

Down on the cor - ner, out here in the street, _ Wil-ly and the

Repeat and fade

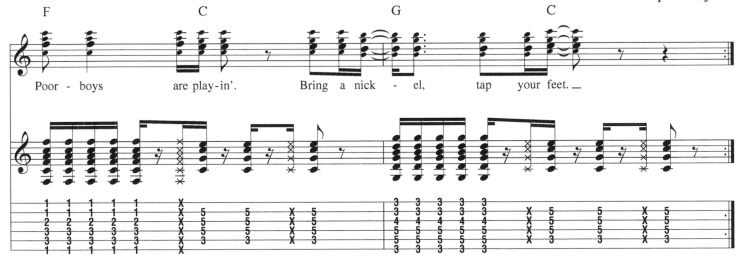

Poor - boys are play-in'. Bring a nick - el, tap your feet. _

Additional Lyrics

2. Rooster hits the washboard, people just gotta smile.
   Blinky thumps the gut bass and solos for a while.
   Poorboy twangs the rhythm out on his Kalamazoo.
   Willy goes into a dance and doubles on kazoo.

3. You don't need a penny just to hang around.
   But if you've got a nickel, won't you lay your money down?
   Over on the corner there's a happy noise.
   People come from all around to watch the magic boy.

Fortunate Son

Words and Music by John Fogerty

Tune down 1 step:
(low to high) D-G-C-F-A-D

Intro
Moderately ♩ = 128

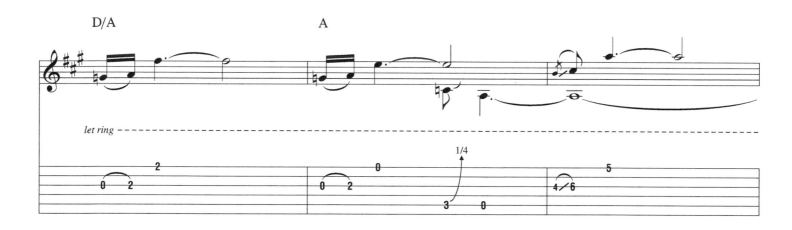

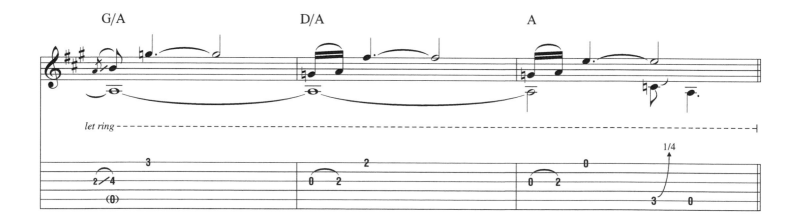

Verse

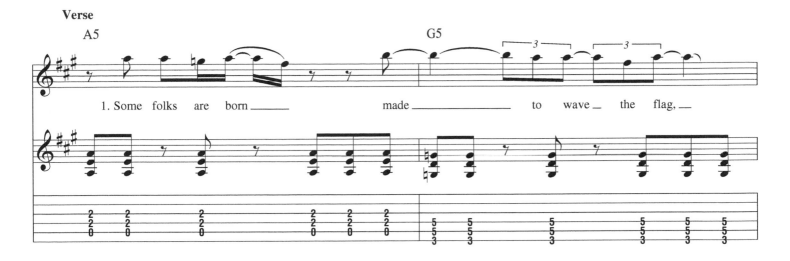

1. Some folks are born _____ made _____ to wave __ the flag, __

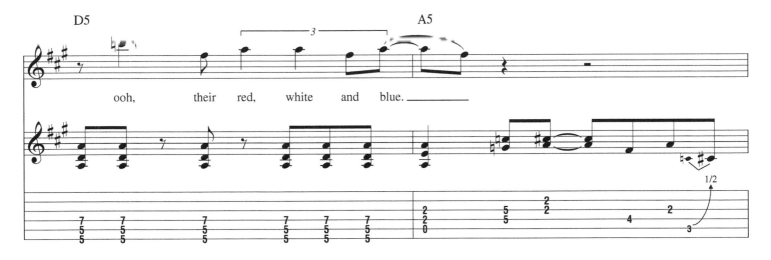

ooh, their red, white and blue. _____

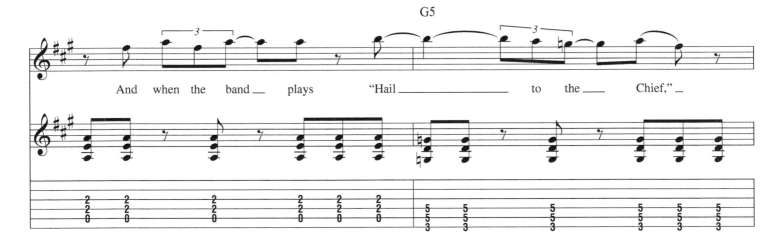

And when the band __ plays "Hail _____ to the ___ Chief," __

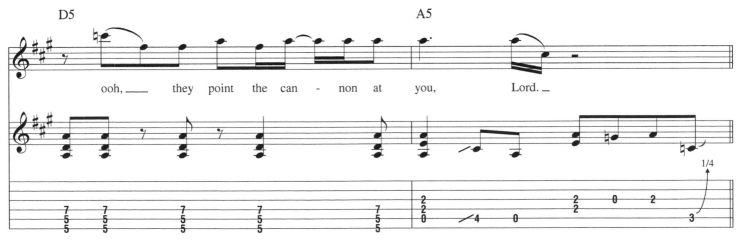

ooh, ___ they point the can - non at you, Lord. __

Chorus

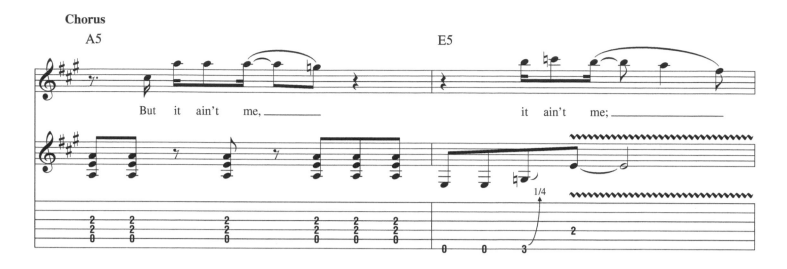

But it ain't me, _____ it ain't me; _____

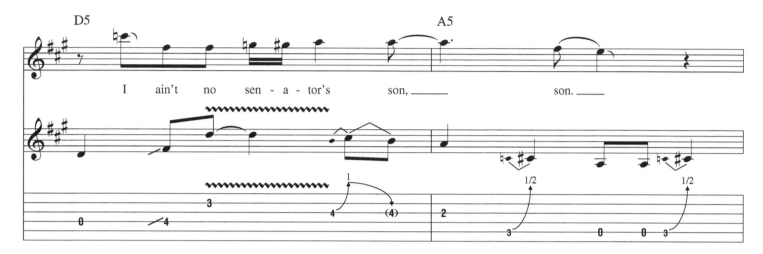

I ain't no sen - a - tor's son, _____ son. _____

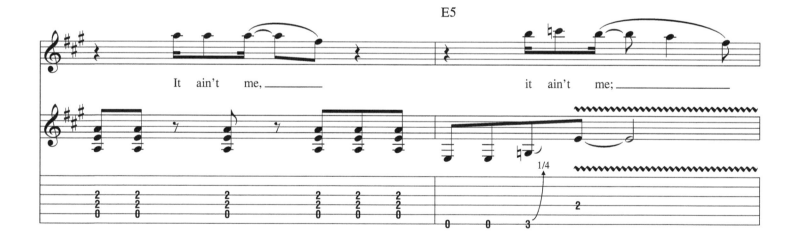

It ain't me, _____ it ain't me; _____

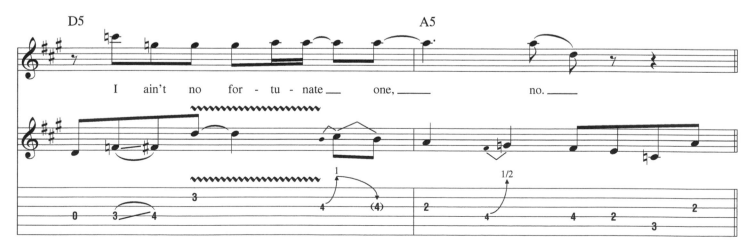

I ain't no for - tu - nate ____ one, _____ no. _____

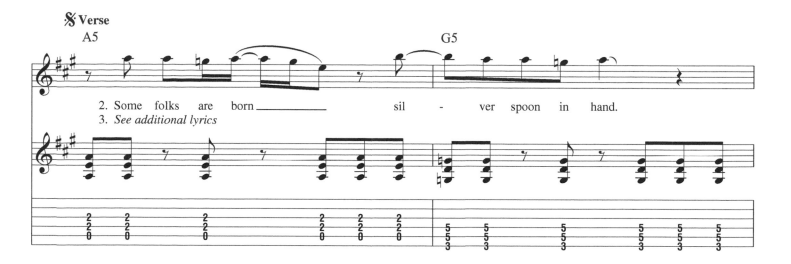

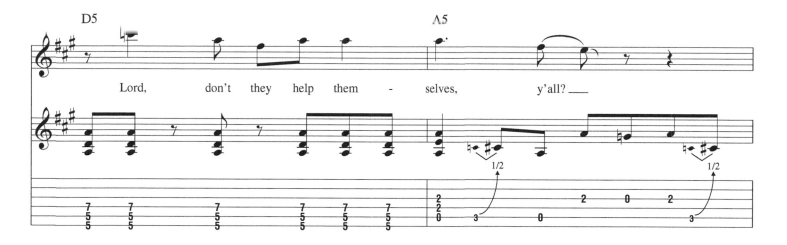

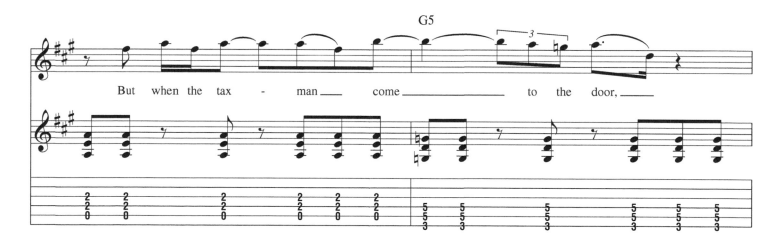

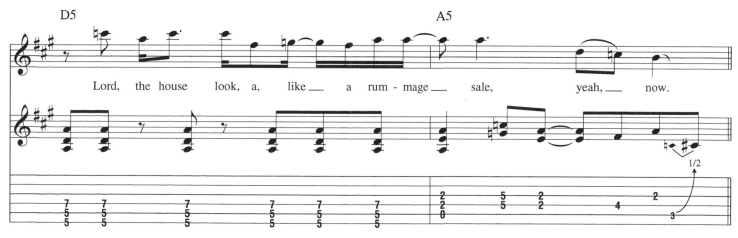

Chorus

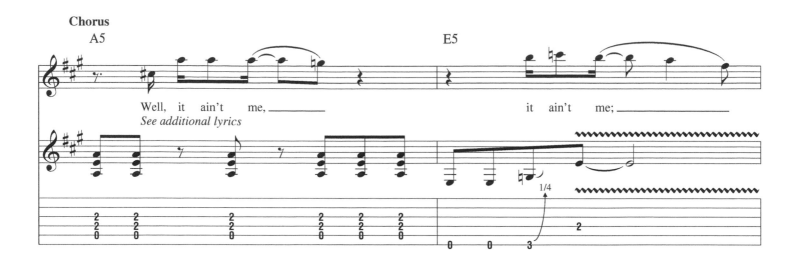

Well, it ain't me, _____ it ain't me; _____
See additional lyrics

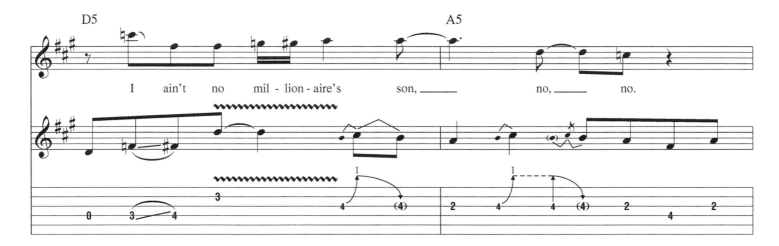

I ain't no mil - lion - aire's son, _____ no, _____ no.

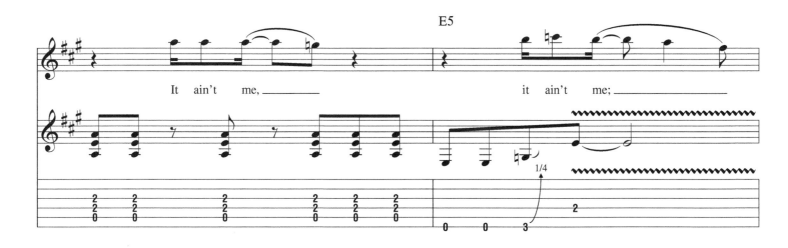

It ain't me, _____ it ain't me; _____

To Coda ⊕

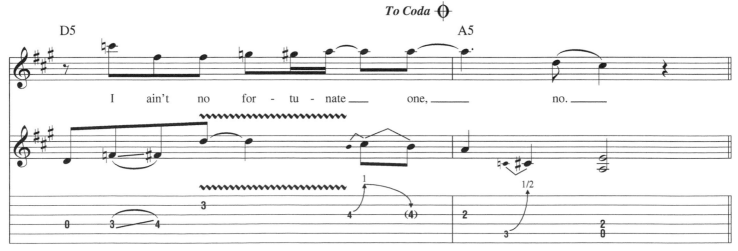

I ain't no for - tu - nate _____ one, _____ no. _____

Interlude

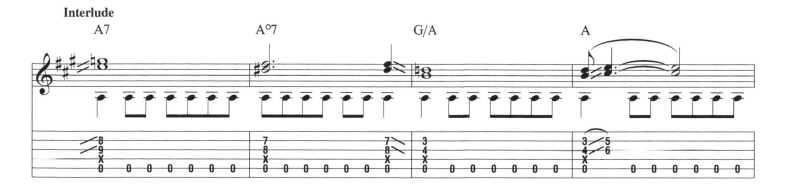

D.S. al Coda

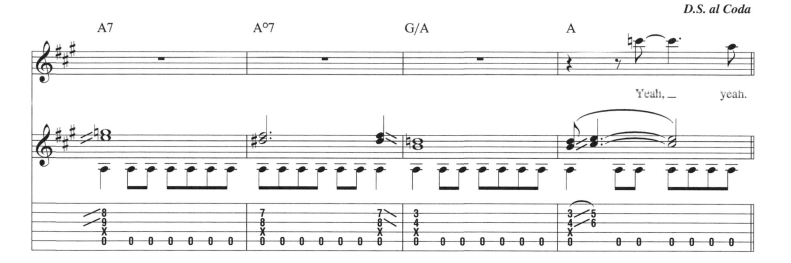

Yeah, __ yeah.

Coda

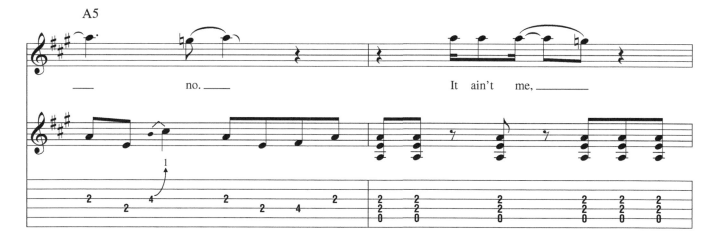

__ no. __ It ain't me, ____

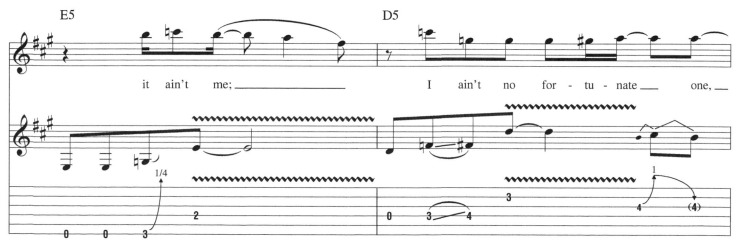

it ain't me; ____ I ain't no for-tu-nate __ one, __

Begin fade

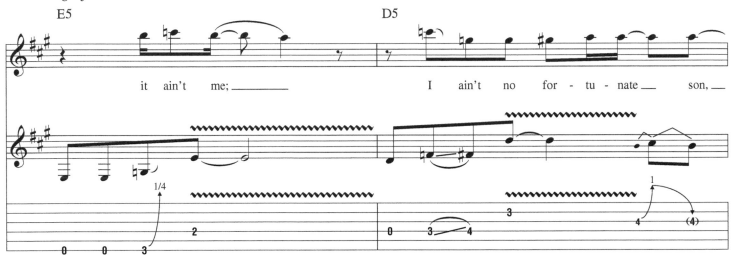

Fade out

Additional Lyrics

3. Some folks inherit star-spangled eyes.
   Oo, they send you down to war, y'all.
   And when you ask 'em, "How much should we give?"
   Oo, they only answer, "More, more, more," y'all.

Chorus It ain't me, it ain't me; I ain't no military son, son, boy.
   It ain't me, it ain't me; I ain't no fortunate one, no.

Green River

Words and Music by John Fogerty

Intro

Moderately ♩ = 138

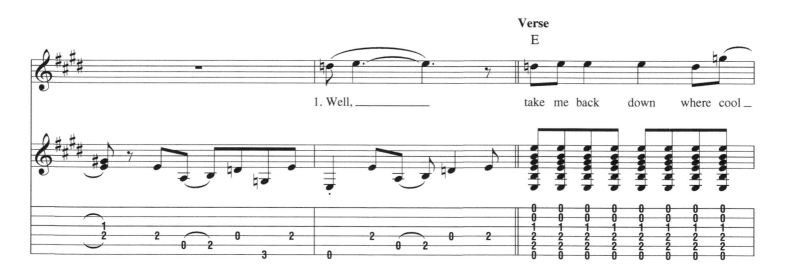

Verse

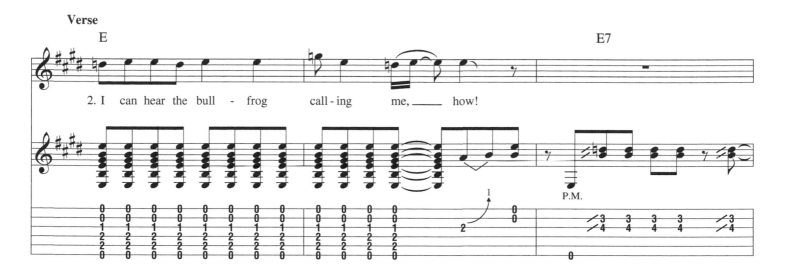

2. I can hear the bull - frog call - ing me, ____ how!

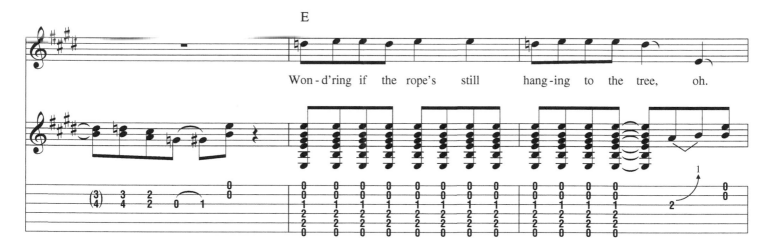

Won - d'ring if the rope's still hang - ing to the tree, oh.

Love to kick my feet way down __

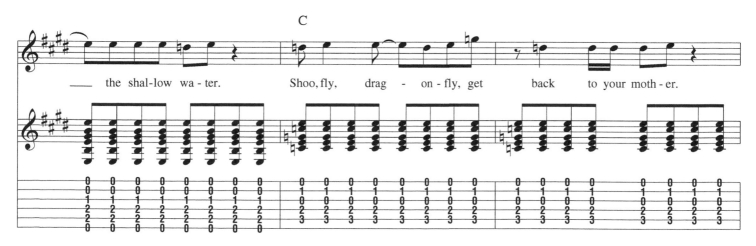

____ the shal - low wa - ter. Shoo, fly, drag - on - fly, get back to your moth - er.

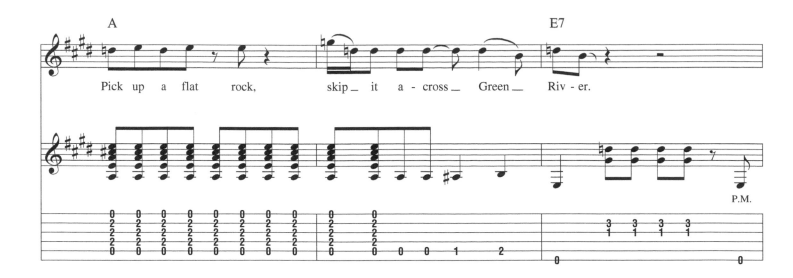

Pick up a flat rock, skip it a - cross Green Riv - er.

Guitar Solo

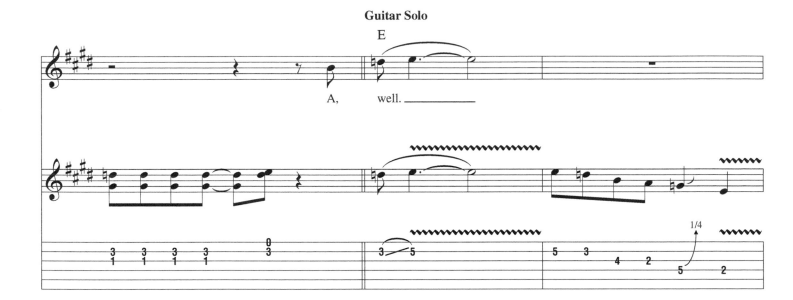

A, well.

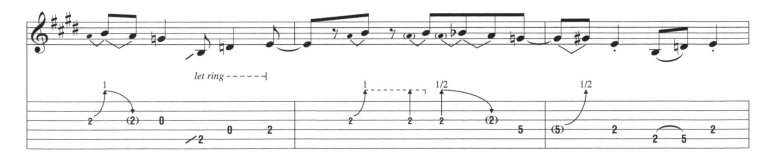

Verse

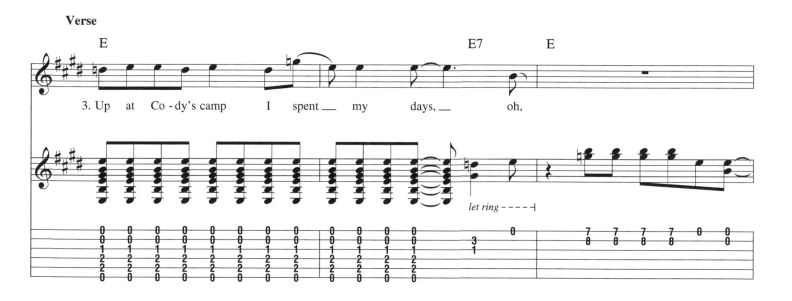

3. Up at Co - dy's camp I spent __ my days, __ oh,

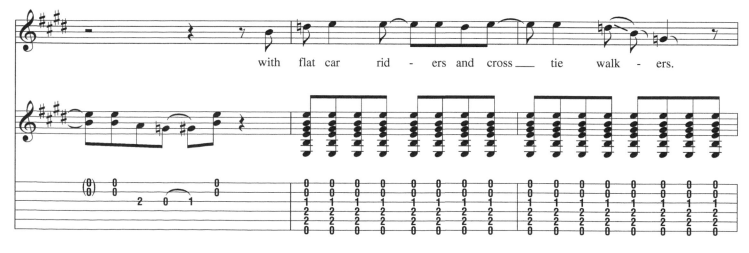

with flat car rid - ers and cross __ tie walk - ers.

Old ___ Co - dy Jun - ior took ___

C

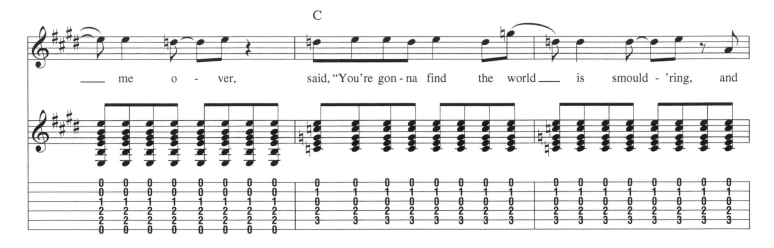

___ me o - ver, said, "You're gon - na find the world ___ is smould - 'ring, and

A   E7

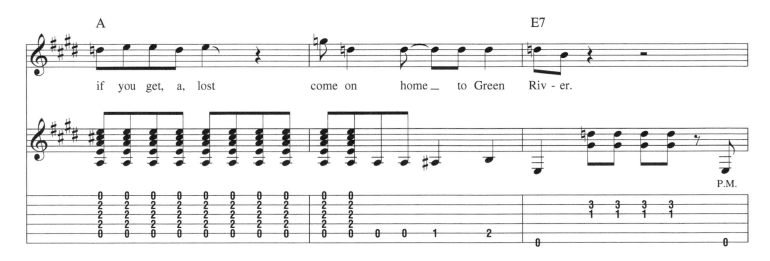

if you get, a, lost   come on   home ___ to Green Riv - er.

P.M.

Outro-Guitar Solo

E

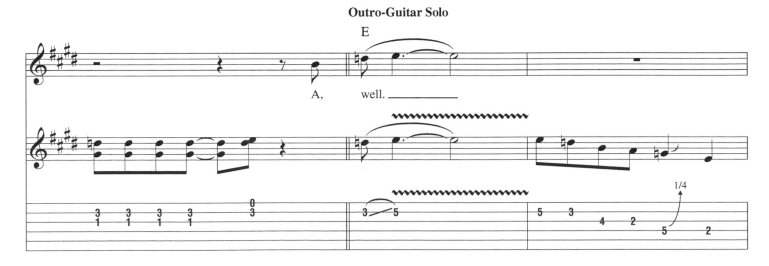

A,   well. _____

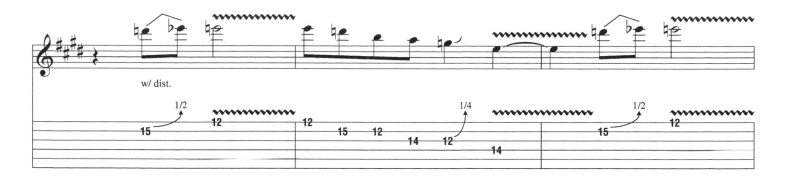

w/ dist.

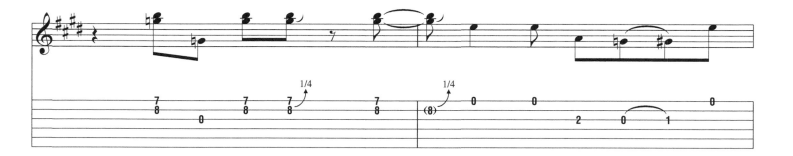

Begin fade

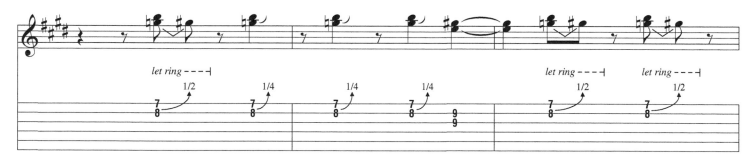

Fade out

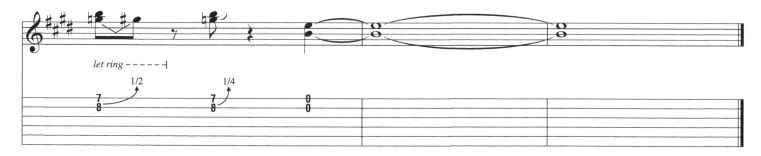

Lodi

Words and Music by John Fogerty

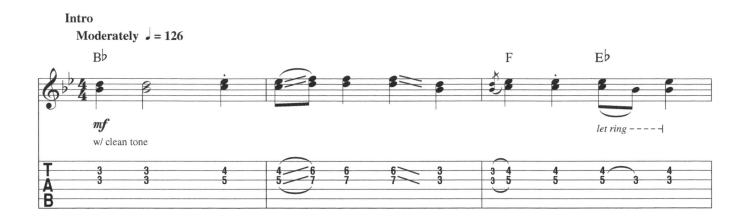

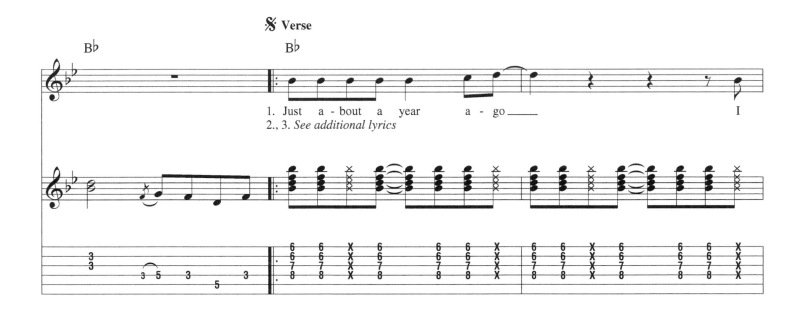

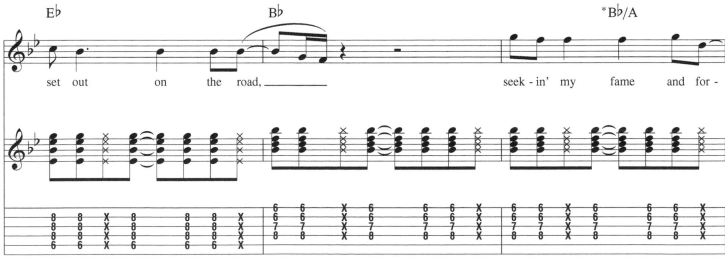

*Bass plays A.

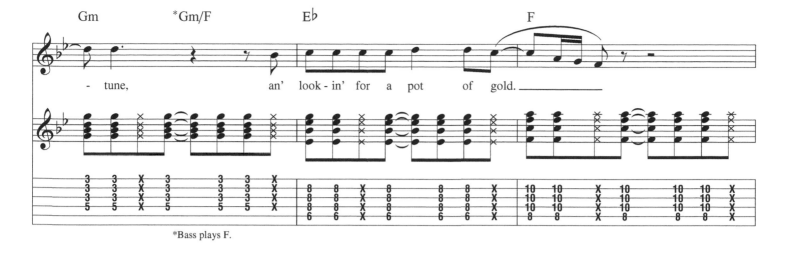

*Bass plays F.

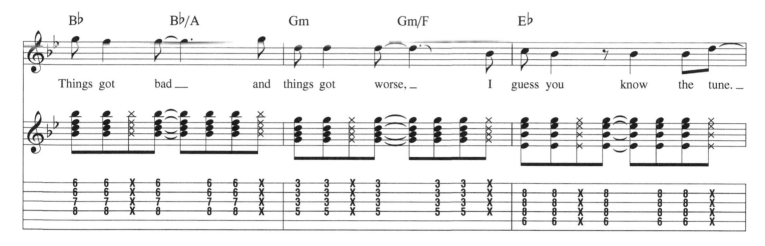

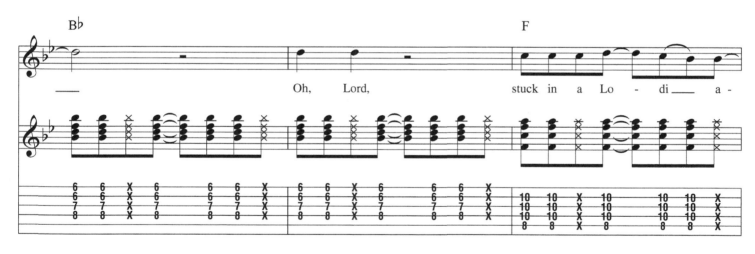

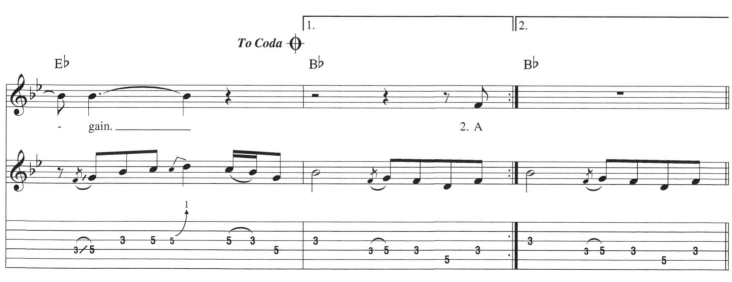

Interlude

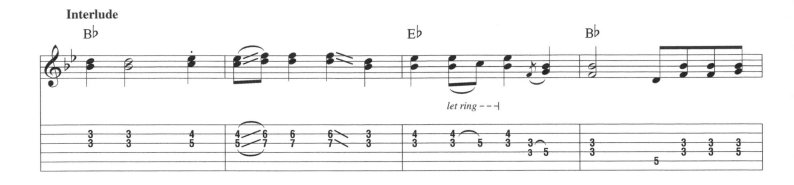

D.S. al Coda

3. The

⊕ **Coda**

Interlude

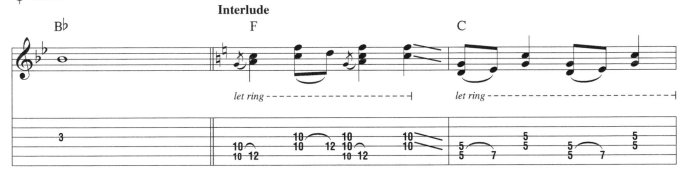

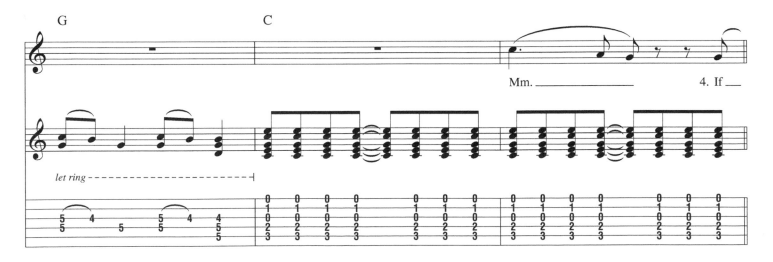

Mm. _____ 4. If ___

Verse

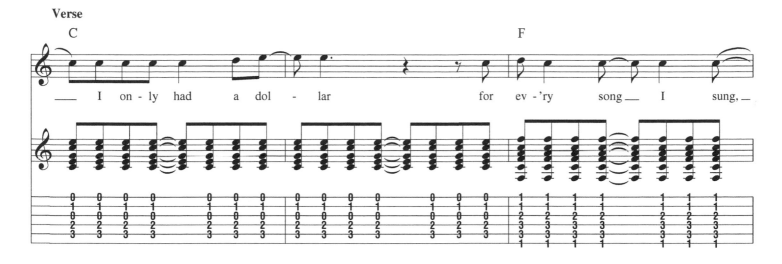

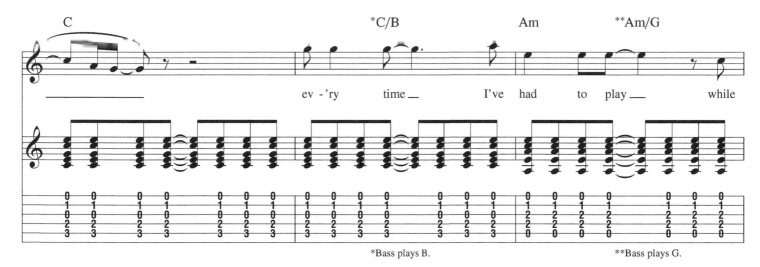

*Bass plays B.   **Bass plays G.

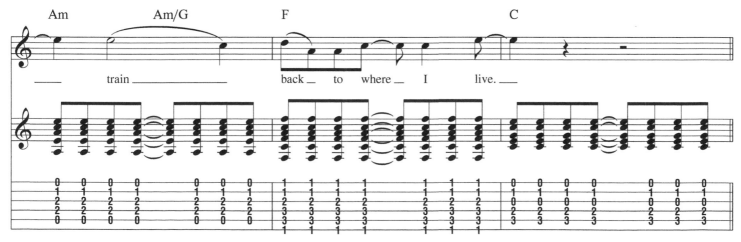

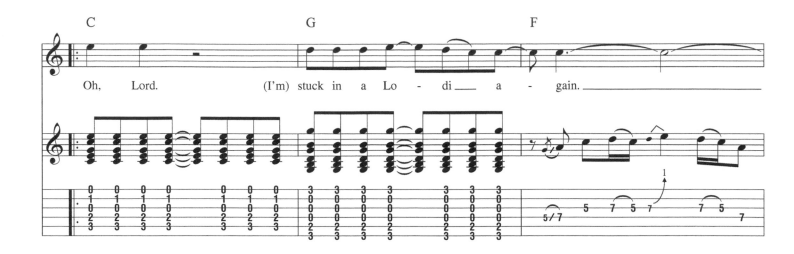

Oh, Lord. (I'm) stuck in a Lo - di ____ a - gain. _____

Outro

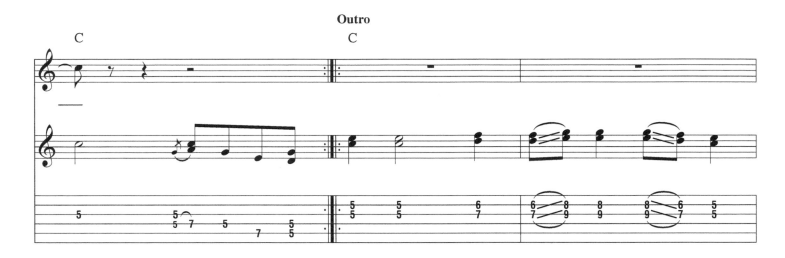

let ring - - - - -|

Repeat and fade

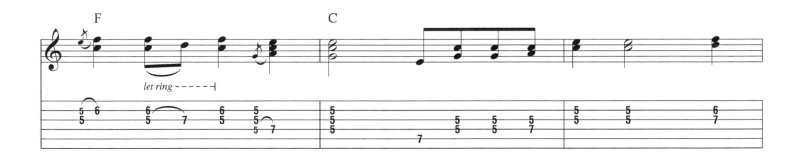

Additional Lyrics

2. A rode in on a Greyhound, well, I'll be walkin' out if I go.
I was just passin' through, must be seven months or more.
Ran out of time and money; looks like they took my friends.
Oh, Lord, I'm stuck in a Lodi again.

3. The man from the magazine said I was on my way.
Somewhere I lost connections, I ran out of songs to play.
I came in to town a one night stand, looks like my plans fell through.
Oh, Lord, stuck in a Lodi again.

Proud Mary

Words and Music by John Fogerty

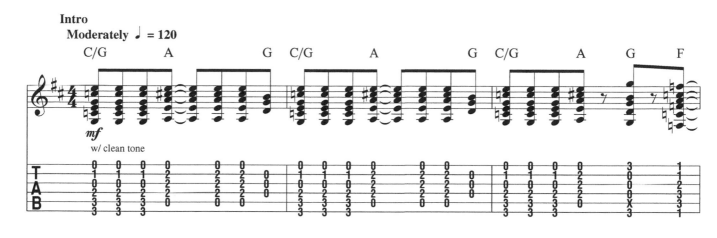

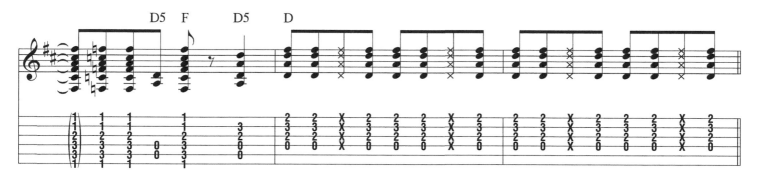

1. Left a good job in the cit - y,
2., 3. *See additional lyrics*

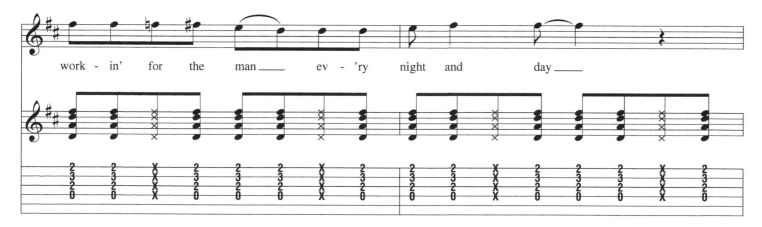

work - in' for the man ev - 'ry night and day

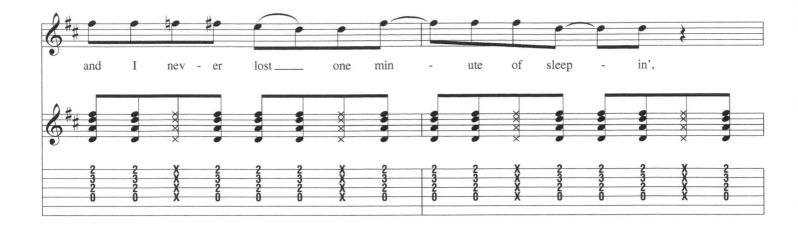

and I nev-er lost____ one min - ute of sleep - in',

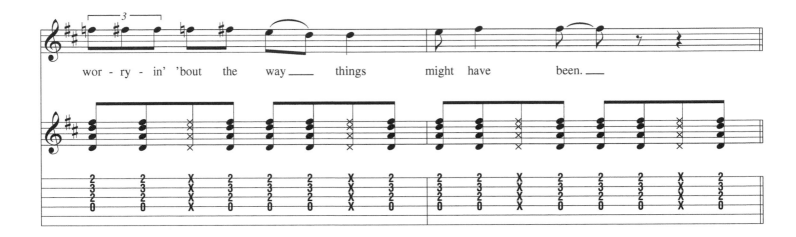

wor - ry - in' 'bout the way____ things might have been.____

Pre-Chorus

2nd & 3rd times, substitute Fill 1

A   Bm

Big wheel_ keep on turn - in', Proud_ Mar - y keep on burn - in'. Roll-

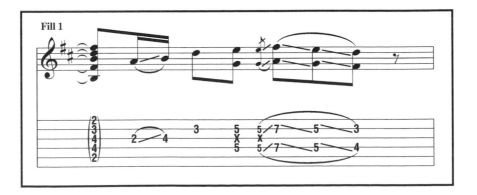

Fill 1

Chorus

-in',   roll - in',   roll - in' on a riv - er._____

Interlude

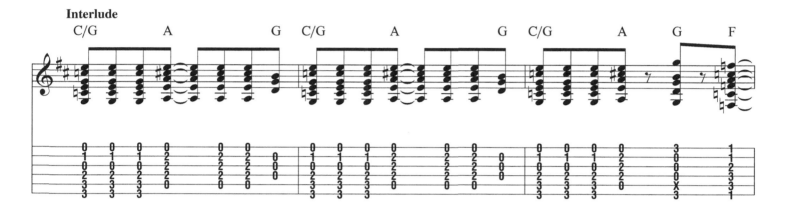

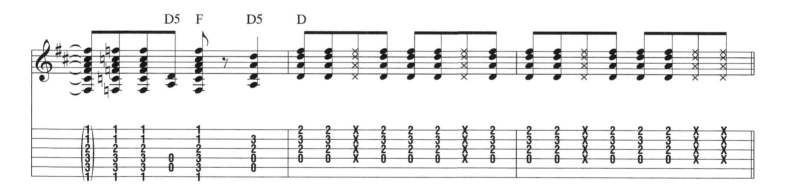

Guitar Solo

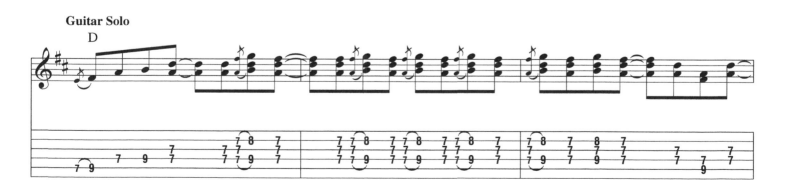

Bm

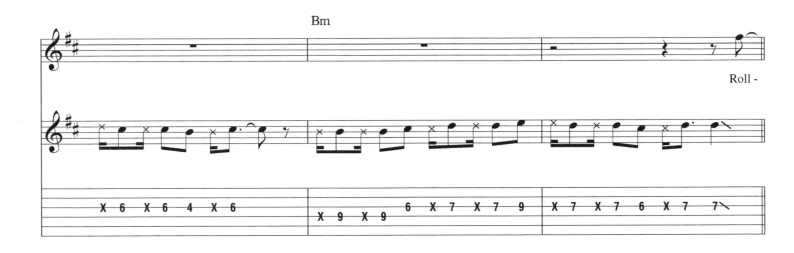

Roll -

D.C. al Coda

Chorus

D

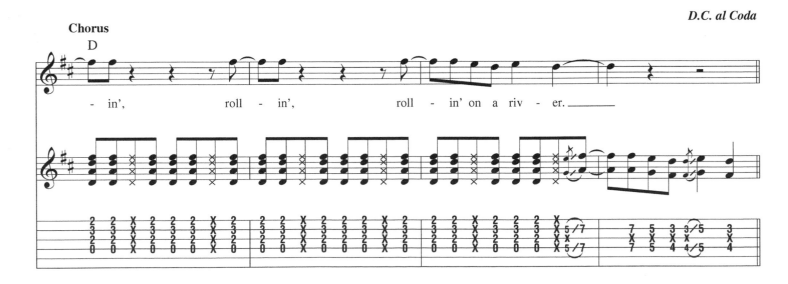

- in', roll - in', roll - in' on a riv - er. _____

Coda

Outro

Roll - in',   roll - in',   roll -

Repeat and fade

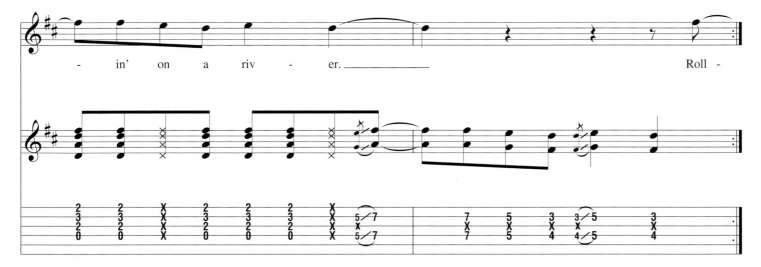

- in' on a riv - er. _____   Roll -

Additional Lyrics

2. Cleaned a lot of plates in Memphis,
   Pumped a lot of pain down in New Orleans,
   But I never saw the good side of the city
   Till I hitched a ride on a riverboat queen.

3. If you come down to the river,
   Bet you're gonna find some people who live.
   You don't have to worry 'cause you have no money,
   People on the river are happy to give.

Up Around the Bend

Words and Music by John Fogerty

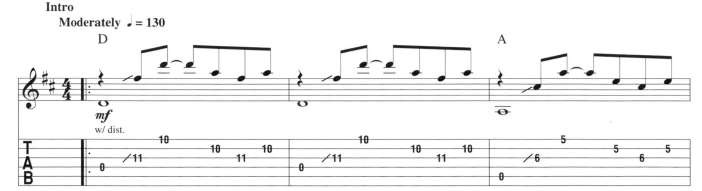

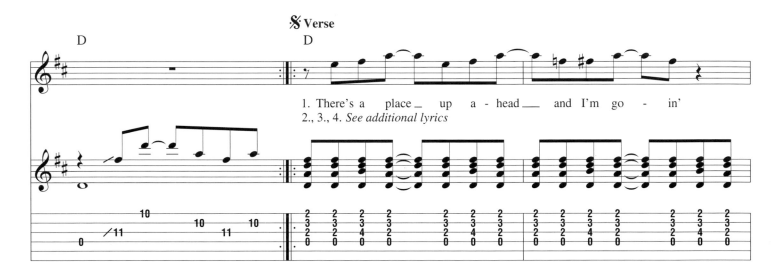

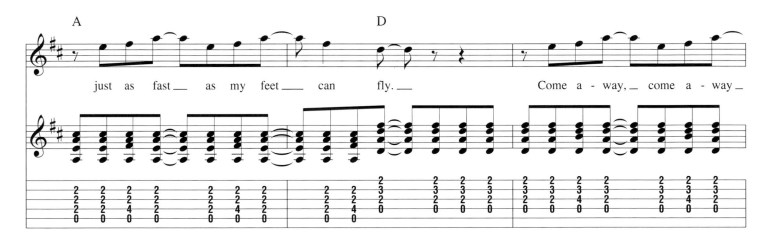

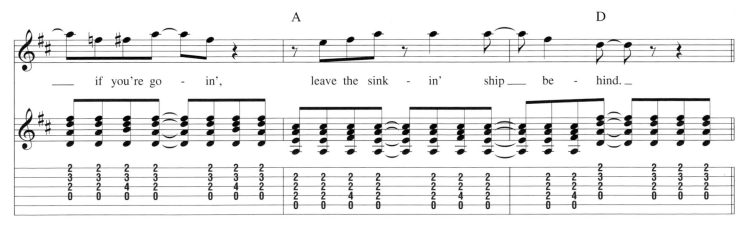

Chorus

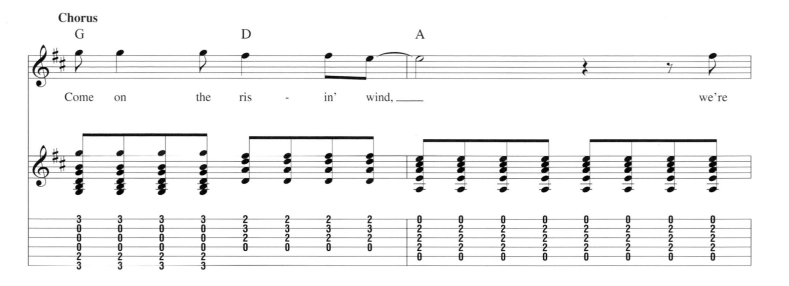

Come on the ris - in' wind, _____ we're

4th time, To Coda ⊕

Play 3 times

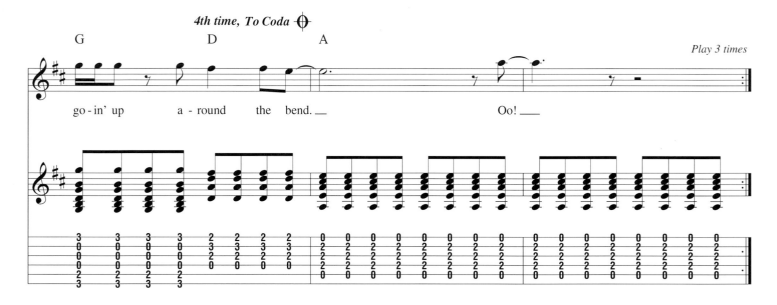

go - in' up a - round the bend. __ Oo! __

Interlude

Guitar Solo

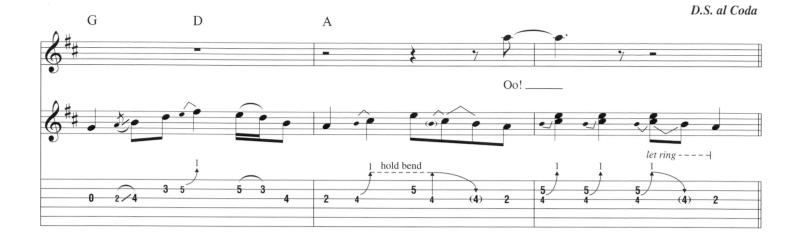

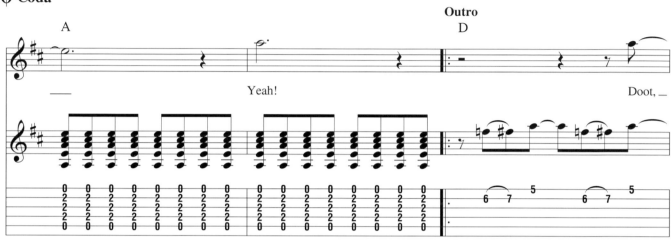

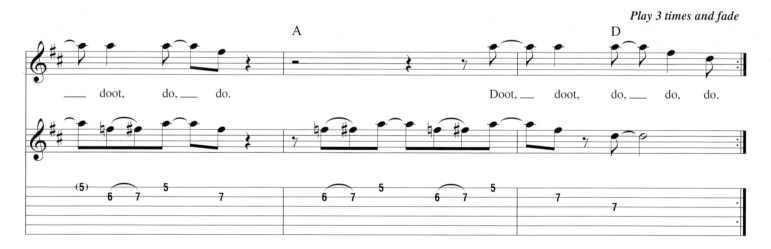

Additional Lyrics

2. Bring a song and a smile for the banjo.
   Better get while the gettin's good.
   Hitch a ride to the end of the highway
   Where the neons turn to wood.

3. You can ponder perpetual motion,
   Fix your mind on a crystal day.
   Always time for a good conversation,
   There's an ear for what you say.

4. Catch a ride to the end of the highway
   And we'll meet by the big red tree.
   There's a place up ahead and I'm goin';
   Come along, come along with me.